shadows of light

k. buehler

| shadows of light |

shadows of light.

copyright © 2024 by k. buehler.

all rights reserved.
printed in the United States of America.
for information, address
401. E. Manning Ave.
Ottumwa, Iowa 52501

k. buehler books are published by
No Opportunity Wasted (NOW), LLC.

co-creators
art contibutors: o. hernandez norris | d. dominguez
editors: m. carson | n. krause

ISBN: 979-8-9907284-1-7 (trade paperback)
ISBN: 979-8-9907284-0-0 (ebook)
first edition: May 2024

10 9 8 7 6 5 4 3 2 1

| shadows of light |

| shadows of light |

essence

him   pg #1

her   pg #96

| shadows of light |

| shadows of light |

him
(the many shades of them)

| shadows of light |

your soul touched mine
with whispers at night
waiting to be seen
ready to be heard
you now live in the ink
that fills these pages
with shadows of light

| shadows of light |

i wish i could move on from this
our horizons meet worlds apart
our skies bleed as our hearts beat

wounds are voids and cosmic chasms
souls are oceans and glass reflections
our sunsets shattered into dusk
daggers of love trigger healing

suspended between indifference and hate
love held me as i passed through you

| shadows of light |

almost tried
almost said
almost started
almost finished
almost quit
almost waited
almost left
almost stayed
almost died
almost lived

| shadows of light |

i don't talk about you
i buried you instead
6 feet under the earth
my heart rots
poisoning my veins
they ask to help
but get angry
when they intercept
my pain
so i reject love
and accept shame

| shadows of light |

the weight of one sided love
is deeply profound
it crushes the heart
souls that dive into the depth
illuminate darkness
and emerge on fire

| shadows of light |

pull me in
like the moon
bids ocean tides
drown me
like the sun
scorches the sky
see through me
like the stars
pierce the night

| shadows of light |

to you
she was
an exotic flower
carelessly picked
to fill an empty vase

to her
you were a
massacre

| shadows of light |

it was my
dark hair
and my
blue eyes
aside from
my dimples
i was
your type
i looked
like her
and she
looks
like me

| shadows of light |

our atoms collide
instantaneous
inevitable
you plus me
toxic chemistry

| shadows of light |

>your heart carries
>the heaviness
>of all the words
>your soul
>aches to speak

| shadows of light |

i would undo
all my plans
for you

| shadows of light |

you are my ex for a reason

without the curve of me)
or the slant of you   /
there would be no ex   )

we crossed the line

| shadows of light |

slowly
you mixed your bleach
with my brilliance
you watched
as my colors bled
suddenly
i was lifeless

| shadows of light |

maybe you feel like home
because i rested my head
in a bed of broken dreams
your illusion became reality

| shadows of light |

why do you
bring me close
when you're
in pain
or drowning
in darkness

yet
push me away
in the light of day

| shadows of light |

after you left
darkness consumed me
filling every part
of my being
shadows of death
bled from my eyes
thoughts of you
crushed me violently
i escape life when
i fall asleep
the reality is
you will never
wake up

| shadows of light |

young death
who is to blame
i knew you were
hurting, lost in pain
looking back, we never
really talked about
that time you called
i answered knowing
you wanted to die
i listened with love
while you quietly cried
now that you're gone
and i'm still here
i still don't talk about
that time you didn't call
you stole my chance
to answer
and my choice
to listen
your death happened
and i'm still here
i carry this pain and
live with the blame

| shadows of light |

the sun comes up
but it's still dark
the baby still cries
but sounds mute
the car drives
but still doesn't move
the pain still hurts
but i feel numb
now that you're gone
everything is the same
everything is different

| shadows of light |

if you could come back
would you still want to die?

| shadows of light |

there is a trace of you
in every touch
in every dream
in every bed
in every kiss
in every shadow
in every memory
please leave
i'm done sharing
space with you

| shadows of light |

you claim to be a monster
i see a beautiful misfit
the dissonance of your song
caused them to shy away
it's not wrong, just different
my curiosity, stronger than fear
i shivered with pleasure
approaching the erotic unknown
exploring untamed elements of you
my soul called to the forbidden

a beast surviving in shadows
indifferent to life and love
i tasted all of your dark
you drank in all of my light
this is how we began
i loved the monster and the man

| shadows of light |

you grow flowers
in the darkest
parts of me

| shadows of light |

i felt your soul
embraced your pain
reflected your beauty
cherished your flaws
i would have loved you
for a lifetime
    but
you let me go

| shadows of light |

you remind me
of the home
where i grew up
unstable, unsafe
empty cupboards
full of anger
love shadowed
with hate

he reminds me
of the home
i dreamed of

| shadows of light |

the elephant in the room
your soul silently speaks
you captured my heart
like i wish he could
will there be a day
i don't apologize for
what i feel

| shadows of light |

i write poems and ask what you think
you let your silence speak

| shadows of light |

your act of
silence
betrays your
soul

| shadows of light |

loving you is
like speaking words
without letters and
singing songs
without sound

| shadows of light |

my soul is home
to a beautiful oasis
drawn to the warmth
of my soft shores
i welcomed you
to my island of bliss
you marveled and wondered
at the fruit in my gardens
you drank deep from my rivers
found refuge in my shade
absorbing your pain
i got consumed by passion
my soul slowly dying
my dirt became dust
those cracks became wounds
the path of you
led to my destruction
you pillaged my eden
then ran from the ruins
your soul fades
like footprints on shores
while i heal from the toxin
that poisoned
my inner paradise

| shadows of light |

>you and me were
somewhere between
one night stands
and happily ever after
codependent at best
toxic at worst

| shadows of light |

i broke
my heart
to set
yours free

| shadows of light |

my scars hold stories
that would shatter
your fragility
i don't want pity
so i let you touch
and never share

| shadows of light |

i didn't know déjà vu
until i met you

| shadows of light |

you say the heart
wants what it wants
then beat it
into submission

you dream of
touching the
universe

while she waits
to taste your
lips

| shadows of light |

you're the best gift
i ever received
but didn't get to keep

| shadows of light |

when we say
"i love you"
i think we mean
different things

| shadows of light |

you speak
your truths
and i wish
they were lies

| shadows of light |

he got love
filled with
shadows of you

| shadows of light |

you asked me
to come
so i did

i imagined staying
so i left

| shadows of light |

i will always be
your greatest love story
just not the one you
lived out loud

| shadows of light |

our love feels like
what movies
are made of
yet there's
no lights
no camera
only inaction

| shadows of light |

my heart collapses
on itself
caged inside my chest
my legs shake
trying to stand
it takes everything in
me to want to live

| shadows of light |

without our magic reality is mediocre

| shadows of light |

maybe i should
appreciate the idea
of being your dream
not your reality

| shadows of light |

                    dehydrated from a thirst
                     you promised to quench
                      you awakened a flame
                        you could not feed

| shadows of light |

beneath the sheets
you preyed

scorching my skin
to satisfy your lust

i hated myself
until i realized

i was a sacrifice

to satisfy
your pleasure

| shadows of light |

we played
go- fish and slap jack
when we were kids
but stakes are higher now
loving you was a gamble
you held cards
in front of a face
i could never read
believing your silence
was a bluff

i called

you raised

my heart wasn't
the only thing lost
in the games
that we played

| shadows of light |

i start to forget
my need to forget you
when i walk into
the library downtown
memories flood
i feel your touch
my heart thunders
my lips tingle
then i remember
the reasons why
i choose to forget you

| shadows of light |

                                        i cringe at your touch
                                          because of his

| shadows of light |

sometimes you hear
the perfect song
one you'd like
to share with her
then you remember
that she's gone
sometimes she's
the only thought
that occupies your mind
that's because your music
made beautiful memories

| shadows of light |

you were a friend
i would call
at midnight or one
to get the job done
then i'd go home
i liked being alone
those nights were fun
you accessed everything
except my heart
your touch took me
to places unknown
uninhibited, euphoric pleasure
we bathed in holy water
until one night
we made love
instead of having sex
suddenly the ocean in you
suffocated the fire in me
friends can become lovers
but lovers can't be just friends

| shadows of light |

i silenced your sound
burying memories deep
i pushed you under
so i could breathe
then you resurfaced
erupting like rivers
of fire searing through
the center of my chest

| shadows of light |

you live in a corner
sitting in the dark

like a child in time out

you sulk in silence
shadows are your sound

I'm guilty

| shadows of light |

so much of our story
i can't recall
distinguishing truth
from the lies
is like sorting
water from fog

| shadows of light |

you're gone
yet echo
in the chambers
of my heart

| shadows of light |

you felt like heaven
until you branded me
with scars from hell

| shadows of light |

your eyes are heavy
with toxic desire
fading to sleep
recalling those memories
i wish you'd forget
you consume my body
until morning invades
hard and horny
you cum in her
while imagining me
the baby cries
so you make a bottle
while you numb yourself
with another drink
isolated in fantasy
you conjure me
taking control without
my knowledge or consent
you stroke yourself
with my hands
and drain her dry
we are both victims
unwilling yet complicit
in your erotic illusion
sober up
get a grip
you are losing her
and can't have me
welcome back to reality

| shadows of light |

why am i waiting on you
to give me everything
he is begging me to take

| shadows of light |

dignity, safety, pleasure
softly, slowly
we built intimacy
gentle whispers
quiet strength
this love resonates

| shadows of light |

you feel like dead weight
struggling in silence
you wound yourself
suffering alone
you justify the torture
because you're afraid
to burden others
with the hate
you hold for yourself

| shadows of light |

when i looked inside
your beautiful soul
i saw a cage
disguised as a garden
roses of rejection
wounded waterfalls
stagnant streams
paths of pain
fences of abuse
i touched a petal
tasted the poison
of your self-hatred
i wish i could free you
from the prison
of your mind

| shadows of light |

i should have
been cautious
but i was
too surprised
you came back
into my life

like turbulence
on a flight
i should have
thought twice

| shadows of light |

you and i
make art together
traversing space
transcending time
i paint with sound
you color with silence
we both create
i hear in shades
you taste in sound
the waves of you
mixed with
the shock of me
is eternity

| shadows of light |

your choice made mine easy

| shadows of light |

i moved to colorado
for mountains
and adventure
you stayed in iowa
for bandmates and
lonely love songs
when i headed west
my heart remained
with a blonde drummer
wearing blue eyes

| shadows of light |

you wish their
soul could touch
yours like mine

| shadows of light |

i am the light
on your darkest days
an inconvenient shadow
a star illuminating
your darkest truths

| shadows of light |

you went
your way
i went mine
all roads lead
somewhere
i hope love is
what we find

| shadows of light |

                        you whispered to me
                  mysteries of mountains
                       and secrets of seas

| shadows of light |

i just want you to know

i wonder.....
what life might have been
if we said yes to our hearts

but

for whatever reasons
we said no
and that hurts

we were good for a while
and that's all it lasted

i also need you to know
i wonder.....
why you stay with
your yes

while i am
the no
next to you
when life is darkest

| shadows of light |

is it fair to stay
if your fantasy
is running away

| shadows of light |

i am on a different path
don't ask me to take a detour
the space between my legs
is not a pit stop
for you to fill up
when you're on empty
i deserve better than that

| shadows of light |

>
> no more eventually
>
> i found forever

| shadows of light |

i don't know how
to keep a friend like you
one that calls when
no one else answers
one that says
"i care about you a lot"
but struggles with
"i love you"

as much as i want to
i don't know how to
keep a friend like you

a friend that's a secret
seems like a sin
one who doesn't call back
one who takes but doesn't give

would you keep a friend like you

| shadows of light |

>you are that soul
>the one who
>survives
>yet has never
>lived

| shadows of light |

there's more to you
trapped in depths unknown
when i got the invitation
from the well of your soul
i dove down deep
to taste and to see
trust me, it's beautiful

| shadows of light |

when you radiated
the truth of love
i was not ready
to reflect it

| shadows of light |

it's strange how
we hold memories
our history has
two different versions
shared moments in time
yet you have your
version and i have mine

sitting together
in a garden of roses
we watch in silence
some people stop
to inhale their beauty
some people slow down
snagged by a thorn
some people meander
unconsciously gliding by
some people hurry
seeing the start of blooms
i get lost in wonder
watching your petals unfold

| shadows of light |

how did my intention
to stay turn me into
the one that got away

| shadows of light |

                                                  you taught me
                                                    to love the
                                               things i hated
                                               about myself

| shadows of light |

we met
i wasn't ready
until i was
you were ready
until i wasn't

| shadows of light |

>we speak in silence
>your presence is loud

>peace
>acceptance
>oneness
>us

>maybe understanding
>is another word for love

| shadows of light |

i still love you
but it feels different
because i love me too

| shadows of light |

somewhere
on some planet
at some time
in some place
we are together

| shadows of light |

the beauty
in me
reflects
the beauty
in you

| shadows of light |

you are not
damaged
you are not
cruel
you are not
worthless
you are not
weak

you are the
same child
with a
tender heart
and stars
in your eyes

so love without
reason
or false expectation
love without condition
love without fear

give yourself permission
to live while
you're here

| shadows of light |

you were a mirror
that reflected me
when we shattered
i faced my shadow
with love's light
healing the pain
revealed my treasure

| shadows of light |

i don't know where
your pain started
but it traveled
through many people
until one day
it found me

i saw your wound
then spoke the truth
you did to me
what was done to you

i don't know where
your pain started
but it stopped
with me

| shadows of light |

    you
        were
            worth
                the
                    hurt

| shadows of light |

the fault in our stars
all these false expectations
a wrinkle in time
a crease that could never fold
an illusion that pulses
memories gone dark
you let go of my hand
i cut the thread to my heart
you can't mend what is broken
from the start

a red thread sewing us into
this karmic cycle
it looks divine yet
keeps me trapped and bound
suspended in forever
mesmerized by our dance
what was meant to be
brilliant beautiful and bright
darkened by shadows of fear
blinding me with eternal night

through the eye of the needle
the picture sounds clear
i flicker through a flame
a shadow of myself
a complicit composer intoxicated
by the music of our art
staring at my reflection
caused the mirror to crack
so I gazed into the abyss
and let it all go black

we were destined to meet
no happenstance
you played chords of my heart
i had never heard
notes struck, searing my soul

| shadows of light |

with scarlet letters
oblivious to the danger
from the comets you shot
our love burned brighter
with each falling star
that i caught

liberated by threads
of cosmic gold
i travel from future to past
and watch the truth unfold
our star song was silenced
by the voids that i found
blindly listening for your
melody in the chasms
my star dust created
scar wounds
making the sky rain red

it was me who traded
the sun for the moon
drowning myself in
the magical symphony of you
i chose to get tangled
in this karmic web

no more false expectations
no more illusions from the past
healing what is broken
won't allow this cycle to last
strumming new songs
on tender strings
i no longer bleed

my soul soars with rest
my heart drums with peace
i was the song
i searched the universe for

| shadows of light |

you kiss my hand
i feel the crescendo of my heart
you can't mend what was woven
together from the start

| shadows of light |

her
(the many shades of me)

my soul silently asks
"why do you long for love
from people full of pain?"

| shadows of light |

swimming in the ocean of me
my soul is slowly drowning
why does living sometimes
feel so much like dying

| shadows of light |

torn
cut
inked
crumpled
folded
painted
burned
crushed
sliced
used
creased
wadded
recycled
forgotten
my heart feels
like a paper
house

| shadows of light |

far beneath the surface
where i almost drown
i hide myself
afraid to be found

| shadows of light |

maybe you don't fit
because you were
never meant to
exist inside lines

| shadows of light |

why do i believe
love has to hurt

| shadows of light |

believing in him
came at the cost
of trusting yourself

| shadows of light |

why am i warring
for love in a battle
that ended before
it ever began

| shadows of light |

> the one who
> speaks truth
> holds real power
> i'm sorry they
> trusted lies
> instead of
> believing you

| shadows of light |

betraying yourself
to protect him
makes you a traitor
not a martyr

| shadows of light |

>that hole
>in the middle of
>your beautiful heart
>has to be there
>so he can leave it

| shadows of light |

after saving myself
time after time
i finally realized
i don't need rescued

| shadows of light |

avoid
a - void
the abyss
within
we refuse to
acknowledge

| shadows of light |

life has no border
no shorelines
yet i am captive
in the prison
of my mind

| shadows of light |

dear future self,
please choose
yourself
love,
me

| shadows of light |

my understanding of safety
felt like hands that didn't sting
i guess love feels different
when you've experienced abuse

| shadows of light |

the moment you realize
you can't burn the sun
or drown the ocean
you find shade
and learn to swim

| shadows of light |

today is the day
i give myself
what they took

| shadows of light |

loving me gave me
choices
like choosing
how i would hurt
how long i would hurt
and if would risk
being hurt again
loving me gave me choices
like choosing
how i would heal
how much i would heal
and if i would risk
being whole again

| shadows of light |

puzzling over pieces
won't make you whole
it's like reaching
for a hand
that will never
hold yours back

| shadows of light |

authenticity is the language
of the universe
i am not here to be liked
i am here to be me

| shadows of light |

there are parts of you
hiding away
because someone
somewhere thought
it was okay to tell you
parts of you were

too dark
too deep
or too ugly

it was easier for them to judge
easier to separate themselves
instead of trying to understand

sometimes good hearts
choose harmful methods

i am here to tell you
every part of you
deserves to be seen
and to be heard
and be fully accepted
with love and compassion

| shadows of light |

it's hard to fix
your heart
when you
don't know
what's broken

| shadows of light |

i can open
my own doors

| shadows of light |

when you're used to starving
lack of hunger feels wrong
so you feast on bread crumbs
confusing pain with pleasure
you drink from dry cups
pouring salt in your wounds
decline invitations, accept demands
you mistake love for lust

forgive yourself

one day the illusions will shatter
you will invite love in
honey will heal your wounds
wine will fill your cup
you will feast until you're full
love lets you choose

| shadows of light |

with each beat
your shattered heart
splinters through you
like broken glass
that unresolved trauma
fractures your soul
search the shadows
go gently to the dark
resolve the pieces of the past
and heal the present
you deserve to feel a heart
with a whole beat

| shadows of light |

u - n - verse
universe
you - in - verse

you are a
sacred sound
and a cosmic note

| shadows of light |

it takes time
to let go of
certain people
their absence
feels significant
right now
lack of presence
feels unbearable
one day you'll
discover you forgot
the way they felt
you think less of
them and move
gently toward yourself

| shadows of light |

                                        curiosity is not love

| shadows of light |

you are careful because
you were handled carelessly
you are cautious because
your heart was broken
so you trip and fumble
i understand your fear
so i will never judge you
i will never condemn you
each mistake is an attempt
to inch closer to whoever
stands in front of you

| shadows of light |

when did i start
associating guilt with pleasure
my skin shouldn't crawl with shame
every time we touch

| shadows of light |

when your heart shatters
and leaves someone unaffected

it's not love

| shadows of light |

i can't receive love
until i give it to
myself

| shadows of light |

i searched for love
as it coursed
through my veins
like a raging river
as it beat in my chest
like an ancient drum
it was me
i am truth
i am love

| shadows of light |

                            solitude
                      soul - i - tude
                             the art
                           of loving
                    your whole self

| shadows of light |

i drank the poison
others poured
my soul dissolved
the toxins while
my heart released
the cure

| shadows of light |

you can't fix
someone that
collects pieces
of hearts
they've broken

| shadows of light |

arguing with silence
is impossible
let it speak
so your heart
can listen

| shadows of light |

set healthy boundaries
you deserve to experience
liberating levels of reciprocity

| shadows of light |

when i feel
i can't stay
for myself
i stay for the
song i will
write to keep
someone alive
on their darkest night
this numbing silence
is just a rest
i remember the music
beating inside me
never actually left

wounded healer
you hold your key
to freedom and wholeness

| shadows of light |

the pain of change
is far less than
that of regret

| shadows of light |

bodies are vessels
for souls

| shadows of light |

a strong love
wrong or right
gives poets
a voice
lines flow
as they create art
of their muse

| shadows of light |

at some point
you started to
reject
hate
and
blame
yourself

at some point
you'll start to
accept
love
and
forgive
yourself

| shadows of light |

to touch
something
real
will help
your wounds
heal

| shadows of light |

                                              not every caterpillar
                                              becomes a butterfly

| shadows of light |

the silence of solitude
brings many gifts
like knowing their choice
gave you the space
to hear the sound
of your own strength

| shadows of light |

>you already hold
>the answers to
>questions you
>have yet to ask

>trust the wisdom
>of your soul

| shadows of light |

one day
you'll feel like
it's time

time to open
the windows
to remove
those blinds
to push back
the curtains

time for shadows
to feel the
warmth of light

those who love
you will wait
take your time

| shadows of light |

anatomy of alchemy
fade out with grace
release what was then
heal what is now
emerge in gold

| shadows of light |

when i touched emotion
i became intimacy
when i heard lies
i became truth
when i saw darkness
i became light
when i felt pain
i became healing
when i trusted vulnerability
i became strength
when i faced death
i became life

| shadows of light |

>the mystery of life
>isn't a problem
>to solve
>it's a reality
>to experience

| shadows of light |

sometimes healing
makes the past scream
sometimes wholeness hurts
uprooting trauma
to make space for love
can feel like self-destruction
let go of what was
surrender to what is
release the hate
let love in

| shadows of light |

you deserve balance
between love and loss

you deserve to know
your experiences don't
reflect your character

you deserve to heal
the ache in your chest
while remembering all
the love you shared

healing is as inevitable
as the heartbreak

you deserve to merge
who you were with
who you've become

without light
there is no shadow

| shadows of light |

| shadows of light |

about the poet

A few people have asked me why use k. buehler as a pen name. I have used a few last names in my life (birth, adoptive, married).

Buehler is a name I hated for a long time. The name I associated with so much pain. The name I blamed for being hurt, abused, neglected, hated, feeling anxious, emotionally detached, unworthy, (insert all other trauma and associated feelings). It is the last name of a father who wasn't ready for a daughter.

Patrick Buehler passed away the week before I left on a solo journey to Mexico in October of 2023. The trip had been planned with the intention to write, rest, and reconnect with me.

When Patrick requested to meet in 2020, after much contemplation and hesitation, I anxiously agreed. It was the first time I had seen him since I five years old, I choose a safe place and gave him date and time. We both showed up and had a good conversation about his past, his struggles with substance use, and the impacts that prison had on his life.

The next time I met him, he was chained to a hospital bed learning he had stage IV lung cancer that had spread to his brain. That day I learned he had a 3 month death sentence from the doctor and was serving a life sentence with and Iowa Department of Corrections. His final wish was to not die in prison (I helped get him out) before he died. While writing his obituary, I found out his life dream was to fish in the Caribbean....

On my "solo" trip, I went fishing for the first and last time with my birth dad and released his ashes into the depths of the Caribbean Sea. As he was carried away, I felt each wave release the heaviness of years of accumulated pain and hurt.

I thanked the man who gave me my first last name for living then sent up a prayer that his soul would rest in peace knowing his dream came true.

For the first time, I felt love and an overwhelming compassion for the part of me I have hated for most of my life.

A distant cousin contacted me after I returned and told me the Buehler family tree is full of writers, poets, artists, and creatives. He encouraged me to continue writing to heal and that my writing would be a source of healing for others. This creative endeavor was an invitation to authenticity, vulnerability, and bravery. I accepted and dived into the depths of my soul through poetry to understand myself.

I found beauty in the ashes of past. I reclaimed my voice, my birthright, and my birth name. Letter by letter, word by word, I was reminded that in my darkest moments, love has always illuminated my path and guided me through the shadows and into the light.

In poetry, we find solace, we find beauty, and above all, we find ourselves. Poetry invites us to dive into the depths of our souls where shadows and light dance in eternal harmony. My hope is that we feel the depth of the pain we experience so we might feel the wholeness of healing.

Made in the USA
Coppell, TX
09 February 2025